FAIRIES

Avril Rodway

The Leprechaun Library
published by
G.P. PUTNAM'S SONS
NEW YORK

DO YOU WANT TO SEE THE FAIRIES?

The best qualification for seeing the Little People is to have 'second sight' or be 'gifted'. A 'gifted' person can help you see fairies. Place your foot on his, let him put his hand on your head, look where he points and you will see the fairies. However, if you know no such person, there are certain times of the year and the day which are most propitious to fairy sightings: Midsummer Eve, for instance, or any day at twilight, midnight and the hours before dawn and midday. Some say that it must be 'a very hot day' and that you should be 'just a little sleepy'.

Four-leaf clovers, made into an ointment and rubbed on the eyes, can dispel fairy glamour. Here is a recipe from an early seventeenth-century manuscript for a potion designed to reveal fairies to human beings:

> Put a pint of clear oil with rose-water and marigold water into a glass, and add hollyhock buds, marigold flowers, hazel buds and the flowers of wild thyme – and the thyme must be gathered near the side of a hill where the fairies habitually go. Take grass from a fairy throne and add it to the glass, then leave the glass in the sun for three days. It can then be used.

But do not forget that fairies will often throw dust into your eyes to prevent your seeing them. This is the 'crust' which you sometimes find in your eyes when you wake in the morning.

Fairies are shy, elusive and very private creatures who dislike being spied on. Indeed, they do not like to be referred to directly by their name. For this reason one should refer to them as 'the little people', 'the good neighbours' or 'the good folk'.

One way fairies guard their privacy is by 'shape shifting', by which means mortals are confused as to whether or not they have really seen a fairy. One of the most accomplished shape shifters is Puck, who delights, when in a mischievous mood, in confusing people by taking the shape of a roasted apple in a bowl of ale, or a three-legged stool which disappears when someone tries to sit down on it.

Fairies also mislead men in a more disturbing way. Often a man walking across a marsh or bog at night will follow a bright light which appears to be guiding him. This is the *ignis fatuus* or will-o'-the-wisp and it will leave him stranded in a treacherous bog where his chances of rescue are slight.

Fairies are also great borrowers. They take corn, milk and household utensils from men and are not above taking the grain from standing ears of corn, leaving only the hollow shells behind. Nevertheless, they are in turn generous, for it was the Tobacco Fairy from the Blue Mountains in America who gave the first tobacco seeds to a man to ease his loneliness.

As a race, fairies love cleanliness. They reward good servants by dropping money in their shoes, but slovens are punished by being pinched black and blue. If you want to encourage a fairy to visit you, the hearth should be swept and the fire kept bright. Also, if you leave a bowl of clean water out on the hearth, fairy mothers may come and wash their babies in it.

ENCHANTMENT

Fairy 'glamour' is not what you might imagine it to be. In fairylore it means magic or enchantment and is the spell which fairies cast over mortals to make them see what the fairies wish them to see. Fairy glamour can:

> . . . make a lady seem a knight,
> A nutshell seem a gilded barge
> A shieling seem a palace large
> A youth seem age and age seem youth.
> All delusion, nought was truth.

Fairy glamour is broken by means of a magic ointment, often made of four-leaf clovers. This ointment was often smeared on the eyes of fairy children so that they could see their true surroundings.

One typical story of how fairies use glamour concerns a midwife called upon at night to deliver a baby. On entering the house, she is led to a luxuriously furnished room where the mother-to-be, a very beautiful woman, lies. Having delivered the child, the midwife is asked to smear the baby's eyelids with an ointment. She does this, but accidently rubs one of her eyes with some of the ointment, thereby dispelling the fairy glamour. The house is revealed to be a hovel, the people a group of fairies and the bonny infant she has delivered a misshapen, ugly little creature. As the midwife can now see the fairies, they blind her in the 'seeing' eye and vanish.

THE ORIGINS OF FAIRYLORE

There is no one answer to the question of where fairies originally came from. Some people thought that fairies were the spirits of aboriginal peoples who had been driven out of their homes by a more advanced race. Consequently, in parts of Britain people believed fairies were the spirits of Stone Age men who had been driven underground at the coming of the more advanced Iron Age men.

With the spread of Christianity, people came to believe that the spirits of unbaptised heathens became fairies. These creatures, not good enough for heaven but not bad enough for hell, were held to live longer than men, but having no souls they perished completely when they died.

The origin of fairies has also been explained in a fascinating myth from Iceland. Eve was washing her children when God spoke to her. She hid the unwashed children, and when God asked if all the children were there she said, 'Yes.' Angry that she had lied, God decreed that all the hidden children should remain concealed from mankind forever, and they became the fairies.

People still believe in fairies. Nevertheless, how much easier it must have been in the past to explain mysterious phenomena such as rainbows, shooting stars, the *ignis fatuus* and even the changing seasons as the works of that elusive and unpredictable race, the fairies.

CHANGELINGS

Fairies were often believed to steal human babies from their cradles and substitute their own sickly children. In the past it was considered essential to give unchristened babies as much protection as possible. If they had to be left alone, even for a minute, a lighted candle would be set by the cot or a sprig of mistletoe placed on the coverlet to deter fairy thieves. In some countries, a baby was supposed to be in the fairies' power until it sneezed, and this was eagerly awaited by anxious parents.

Fairy babies were ugly, shrivelled, bloodless little creatures, for as the offspring of spirits they were even less substantial than their parents. Indeed, fairies were so anxious to strengthen their fairy stock that sometimes the substitute 'child' would be just a piece of wood carved in the likeness of a baby. Using 'glamour' the fairies would make the mother think the changeling was her own child, but when the enchantment had faded she would see it for what it was.

A defective human child was often believed to be a changeling put there by the fairies. Many of these poor children were tormented or exposed on a 'fairy hill' or under a 'fairy tree' in the belief that the fairies would take them back again and restore the stolen human young.

However, not all fairy mothers were prepared to abandon their offspring. One poet maintained that fairy mothers had maternal feelings, for 'Wherever yet was found a mother who'd give her baby for another?' Indeed, would the ethereal, spritely fairies be likely to exchange their offspring for 'the dull, helpless sons of clay' that are human beings?

TROLLS

Trolls are fearsome, dwarf-like creatures. Living in caves and mountains, they emerge above ground only to harm people, as this Swedish tale shows.

Once there was a swineherd who owned three fairy dogs. Their names were Hold (who would hang on to anything), Tear (who could pull anything to pieces) and Quick-Ear (who had very sharp hearing). One day the swineherd heard that three princesses had been captured by three evil trolls, and he determined to rescue them. Setting off with his dogs, Quick-Ear soon heard the sound of spinning inside a mountain. Tear tore a hole in the mountainside and revealed the eldest princess. When her enraged captor appeared, the dogs tore him to pieces and the princess was freed. In another part of the mountain the dogs found the second princess, and killing the troll who had captured her, they reunited her with her sister.

But the third troll had discovered his brothers' fate. As the dogs were all thirsty, this cunning troll gave them a drink of water on which he had cast a spell. The dogs were immediately bewitched and, all danger removed, the troll made ready to kill the swineherd. The swineherd begged to be allowed to play one last psalm on his pipe and at the first note the spell was broken. His dogs leaped up and killed the troll.

The third princess now freed, they all returned to the palace. The princesses' grateful father made the gallant swineherd his heir and he married the youngest princess.

FAIRY FEASTS

A roasted ant that's nicely done
By one small atom of the sun;
These are flies' eggs in moon-shine poach'd,
This a flea's thigh in collops scotched.
This is a dish entirely new,
Butterflies dissolved in dew;
These sucking mites, a glow-worm's heart,
This is delicious rainbow-tart.

Few of us would be tempted by the dishes served at this fairy banquet, but fairies enjoy nothing more than holding elaborate feasts followed by singing and dancing. It is perfectly safe for a mortal to attend a fairy banquet and join in the revels. But if you are offered anything to eat or drink, make some polite excuse and refuse. For the choice dish may, in reality, be a dead leaf which has been transformed by fairy glamour, and once eaten it will put you in the fairies' power.

Once a miser provoked the fairies' wrath at a fairy banquet. He was so tempted by the tiny gold and silver plates they ate off that he tried to steal them. In punishment, the fairies tied him up in cobwebs and danced upon him all through the night.

The magic land of Cocaigne or Schlaraffenland also offers bizarre food to the fairies. Here the fairies live in idle luxury. They need make no effort to find food, for the walls of the houses are made of pasties of meat and fish and the roof tiles of wheaten cakes. 'Birds merrily singing, ready roasted' fly into the fairies' hungry mouths and there are buttered larks and garlic a-plenty.

Some fairies live in rivers, lakes and oceans, and stories about them are found throughout the world. The Nicker of Germany live in lakes. These water-sprites, who have green teeth, dance on the water before a drowning takes place. Often they entertain mortals at banquets in their sub-aqueous palaces, but their food tends to be tasteless as they use no salt.

Perhaps the best-known water fairies are mermaids, characterized by their sweet voices, long hair, golden combs and fish tails instead of legs. In many tales they lure sailors to their death.

The mermaid most people know about is Hans Andersen's 'Little Mermaid'. She fell in love with a mortal, a handsome prince, and bargained with a witch to exchange her tail for legs. The price demanded by the witch was the mermaid's tongue. If her prince married her, she would gain an immortal soul, but if not, she would die forever and become foam on the sea. Unfortunately, the prince married another, but the spirits of the air took pity on the little mermaid and made her one of themselves. Her gentle spirit continues to do good to human beings in the hope that she will win her immortality. In Canada, there is a story of a chieftain who found on the shore a beautiful maiden with two fish tails instead of legs. She entreated him to find her a mortal husband so she could obtain a soul: could this have been the same mermaid?

A North American Indian legend tells how one tribe was led long ago from Northern Asia to the coast of America by a Man-fish. This merman had a porpoise-like face, a green beard and, again a pair of fish for legs. It is fascinating to see the similarities between some of these tales from different continents.

Many different types of elves are found in folklore. Some are well-disposed and helpful towards humans. These pert and dapper elves are known as the 'light elves'. They inhabit trees in leafy groves and sometimes, like the Welsh Ellyllon elves, live on so-called 'fairy butter', a fungus which when decayed appears yellow and fatty.

Some elves are malevolent and aptly known as the 'dark elves'. They live deep underground from where they emerge to act spitefully towards humans. If someone appears with 'certain spots, black and blue, as if they were pinched or beaten' you can be sure they have been 'fairy nipped' by the dark elves. They also inflict injuries on cattle and people with their powerful weapon 'elfshot', which consists, in fact, of ancient flint arrow heads. If a cow dies for no apparent reason, and small flat triangular stones are found near its body, country people will believe this to be the work of the elves and their arrows. Elfshot does not kill a man but leaves an irritating rash or spots.

In folklore, people cannot agree what elves really look like. In Denmark they are believed to be hollow at the back while in Scotland the Glastaig elves walk on goats' hooves and have to wear long green dresses to conceal their cloven feet. Perhaps the most reliable description is from Scandinavia, where elves originated: here they are believed to have cows' tails.

FAIRY STEEDS

Horses are among the fairies' favourite creatures. Fairies like their horses to be swift and beautiful and often they give them precious harnesses to wear. Sometimes fairy horses rise out of lakes or rivers, allow men to ride on them for a while, then disappear again beneath the water never to be seen again. It is not unknown for fairies to 'borrow' men's horses, returning them to the stables having ridden them hard through the night. A precaution against this is to plait the horse's mane and tail. Placing a twig of elder in the stable or nailing up an iron horseshoe will also keep the fairies away.

The most usual colours for fairy horses are white, silver and black. A typical fairy horse is Shadowfax in Tolkien's *Lord of the Rings*: 'By day his coat glistens like silver; by night it is like a shade, and he passes unseen. Light is his footfall.' He is devoted to his master and with a speed and endurance far surpassing mere earthly creatures. In contrast the horses of the Ringwraiths, the servants of the Dark Lord, are black, and their speed strikes terror into all who see them.

If you want to ride a fairy horse, look for the fairy plant St John's Wort. If you step on it a fairy horse may well rise from the ground beneath you and let you ride on its back all night. But, be warned, it will vanish in the morning, leaving you to find your own way home.

> They had fine music among themselves and danced in a
> moon-shiny night around or in a ring, as one may see at
> this day upon every common where mushrooms grow.

The magical fairy world is not governed by human time.
Fairies are not troubled by sickness, nor, as spirits, do they age,
and as a consequence they have much leisure for playing. One
of their favourite pastimes is dancing. All kinds of fairies –
from the most grotesque of goblins to the most delicate of
fairies – take part.

An essential ingredient of these dances is good music. In one
tale two fiddlers were offered many pieces of gold to play at the
celebrations of a fairy wedding. They played, without cease,
all night long. In the morning, after they had been paid, the
fiddlers returned to their homes. They then discovered that
not one night but many generations had passed. They began
to age rapidly and within a short space of time they had
crumbled to dust.

In Ireland, another popular and very strenuous fairy pastime is
hurling. Armed with curved wooden hurling sticks, the fairies
delight in this rough game. They often invite humans to take
part because they hope the presence of real flesh-and-blood
men will add a greater strength and vitality to the already
ferocious contest.

FAIRIES IN THE BALLET

Perhaps the fairy image that is most strongly imprinted on the public mind is that of the radiant, quicksilver creature in a froth of pastel net and with tiny gauze wings that we gaze at across the footlights. Costume, lighting and theatrical trickery can make fairies real even for life-long unbelievers.

Sometimes they represent goodness, like the Fairy Godmother in *Cinderella* or the Lilac Fairy in *Sleeping Beauty*, who changes the spell cast on Princess Aurora – by another (wicked) fairy, Carabosse – from death to prolonged sleep. Another famous example, the Sugar Plum Fairy, appears in *The Nutcracker*; the music for her solo, played on the tinkling celesta, is among the best-known pieces in the repertoire.

The sylphide gives her name, in the plural, to a plotless *ballet blanc* to music by Chopin and, in the singular, to an old Bournonville work, *La Sylphide*, which gave Marie Taglioni one of her most celebrated roles and is still popular today. This sylphide is noted for her tantalizing disappearances through windows and up chimneys. Another type of fairy, the water-sprite, is the subject of Frederick Ashton's *Ondine*, created for Margot Fonteyn and very successfully filmed.

Among other ballets based on fairy legends are *Le Baiser de la fée* and *La Péri*, and inevitably there is a ballet version of Shakespeare's *Midsummer Night's Dream*. Called simply *The Dream*, this tells the story of Titania, queen of the fairies, falling in love with Bottom, the weaver, while he is transformed by magic into an ass. All turns out well in the end, however, when Titania is reunited with her rightful partner, Oberon, and Bottom's human appearance is restored.

GOBLINS

Goblins are malevolent little creatures whose appearance, more often than not, is grotesque.

In Christina Rossetti's bewitching poem 'Goblin Market' some of the goblins have faces like cats, owls or rats. Others have tails which they whisk as they tramp along gracelessly, often no quicker than snail's pace. These wicked goblins tempt a young girl, Laura, to buy fruit from them in exchange for a curl of her golden hair. She very foolishly eats the fruit, which tastes sweeter than honey and more intoxicating than wine.

Laura never sees the goblins again, and as she daily grows weaker with longing for this magic fruit, her sister Lizzie determines to get some for her. As the story goes, Lizzie tricks the goblins into squeezing the fruits' juices against her lips. She is careful not to open her mouth, and on returning to Laura she says: 'Hug me, kiss me, suck my juices, squeezed from goblin fruits for you.'

The juice tastes as bitter as wormwood and Laura falls down in a fit. When she recovers she has overcome her longing for the goblins' fruit and lives to tell the tale to her children.

ORIENTAL FAIRIES

There are many fairies to be found in Eastern folklore.

In China, for instance, there are fairies who watch over the household in the same way as the German house elves. One such fairy is Tsao Chen, who protects the house from evil spirits. He is also the guardian of the kitchen or hearth and every year he departs to heaven to report on the behaviour of all the members of the family. It is for this reason that the mouth of his statue is smeared with honey, so that he can speak only sweet words. Another particularly attractive fairy is Ma Ku. This kindly fairy reclaimed a large strip of coastland from the sea and turned it into a mulberry orchard for the benefit of mankind.

Japan, too, has fairies. In common with Europe, they are not referred to directly but called by some people 'little foxes'.

One Japanese fairy maiden wove clothes for the fairy court. Her father, feeling this was no life for a young girl, ordered her to dress herself in some of the clothes she had made and learn to enjoy herself. She did so, and soon fell in love with a shepherd. Thereafter she neglected her weaving completely. Unfortunately, the fairies soon missed having new clothes. They banished the shepherd from the court and the poor maiden returned to her loom. However, in recompense, once every seven days magpies form a bridge in the sky across which she goes to meet her banished lover.

Although fairies might often be benevolent, it was always as well, so people thought, to have some charm or protection at hand to keep them at bay.

Simple protections were a piece of bread, some salt or stones with natural holes in them placed in a pocket. Horseshoes, or anything made of iron, were also effective charms. If none of these were available, alternative means of protection included reciting the Lord's Prayer out loud and whistling. Turning one's coat inside out was also effective and perhaps this is why it is still considered 'lucky' to put on a sock or stocking wrong-side-out. Some plants were considered particularly helpful, such as rowan or any other red-berried plant. Daisies were also powerful deterrents, and this may be why children were encouraged to make daisy chains.

Anyone pursued by wicked fairies or witches could shake them off by jumping over a stream; one flowing from north to south was the best. If the worry persisted, there were always recipes for potions 'against the elfin race and nocturnal goblin visitors'.

> Take the ewe plant, wormwood, bishopwort, lupin, ashthroat, harewort, viper's bugloss, heathberry plants, cropleck, garlic, grains of hedgerise, githrise, fennel; put these plants into a vessel, set them under the altar, sing over them nine masses, boil them in butter and sheep's grease, add much holy salt, strain through a cloth, throw the plants in running water.
>
> Cockayne's 'Saxon Leechdom'

Failing all these, if you held on to your courage and were polite to the fairies you could escape their mischievous attentions.

FAIRY FLORA

> I know a bank whereon the wild thyme blows,
> Where ox-lips and the nodding violet grows;
> Quite over-canopied with luscious woodbine,
> With sweet musk-roses, and with eglantine.
>
> *Midsummer Night's Dream*

These sweetly perfumed blooms, surely the most delightful bouquet of fairy flowers ever known, formed a bower for Titania, the queen of the fairies, where she was lulled to sleep by the sweet songs of her attendants.

Not only do fairies like to be surrounded by flowers but sometimes they choose to live in them. The Elf of the Rose, as his name suggests, made his home in a sweet-smelling pale pink rose where 'behind every petal he had a bedroom'. If you look carefully in the bell of the golden cowslip you may well find a fairy. Speak courteously to this fairy and you will be shown where to find fairy treasure. In Ireland, however, it is under the ragwort flower that you will find the leprechaun's crock of gold.

Not all fairy flowers are beneficial to mortals. If, for instance, you hear bluebells 'ring', you are hearing your death knell. So powerful a fairy flower is the bluebell that many children who once wandered into a bluebell wood have vanished, never to be seen again. And you will certainly offend the fairies if you bring red and white May blossom into your house, for they like to dance beneath it.

THE LORELEI

Many people who have travelled along the river Rhine near Cologne will have had the Loreleiberg pointed out to them. The beautiful creature who gave her name to this rock is popularly depicted as an undine, or water-sprite. According to legend, she used to sit combing her hair on the Loreleiberg, luring sailors to their death by her beautiful singing. On one occasion a brave band of men is said to have tried to capture the Lorelei. Binding them hand and foot by a spell, she threw her jewelled headband into the Rhine, causing the White Steeds of the Flood to rise up and bear her away. The men barely escaped drowning and since then no one has tried to capture the Lorelei.

According to another source, she was a real woman whose beauty drew many suitors. She rejected them all, for she was in love with a knight who had gone to the wars. So many of her suitors committed suicide that people grew to believe she was a witch or evil fairy. She prayed for death, not wishing to be the cause of any more deaths. The Archbishop of Cologne, touched by her story, ordered that she be sent to a convent. On her way there she asked to be allowed to stand on the Loreleiberg for one last glimpse of her knight's castle, and as she stood there she saw her knight returning down the Rhine in a small boat. She called his name and, hearing her cry, he forgot to steer the boat, which was dashed to pieces on the rock. Still calling his name, she jumped into the river to join her knight, and they were never seen again.

THE COURT OF THE FAIRIES

Wherever a fairy court is held – be it in a forest glade, in a hollow hill, or in the eye of an observer bewitched by fairy glamour – it has fired the imagination of artists for hundreds of years.

According to tradition, the high king of all the fairies is Oberon, whose chief courtier, Puck, is always at hand to carry out his commands. Oberon is a very powerful fairy who has the power to control the weather and cause crops to fail. According to Huon de Bordeaux, writing in the fifteenth century, he is only as big as a three-year-old child: the result of a curse laid upon him by a wicked fairy at his christening. Oberon's queen is the beautiful Titania – sometimes known as Mab – and, as

befitting her rank, she is attended by a retinue of maids of honour.

However, each community of fairies is presided over by its own lesser king and queen. One such court is described by William Drayton in his poem 'Nimphidia'. This court is made up of particularly tiny fairies and the queen, Pigwiggen, rides in a coach made out of a snail's shell.

Some fairy courts are made up of trooping fairies whose chief pleasure is to go on 'rades' or ceremonial processions. Sometimes the entire court rides out on tiny white horses which have long manes and sweeping tails. They play music as they go and their green scarves fly behind them in the wind. At other times they proceed on foot, but so light are these fairies that the grass or corn over which they pass is not trodden down, and there is no sign that they have ever been there.

BROWNIES

The brownie is a jolly, cheerful fairy, helpful around the house and on the farm. Indeed, brownies so enjoy human company that they often make their homes beneath human dwellings, where they imitate the behaviour of the humans above.

A brownie will often attach himself devotedly to one member of the family. Nevertheless, he expects some reward, preferably in the form of cakes, honey or bowls of cream. However, any gifts must be left where he can find them for himself and not offered in direct payment.

In common with other fairies a brownie can be put to flight by Christian symbols. In one sad story a brownie fell in love with a lord's daughter, and served her well. She married, and when it was time for the arrival of her first child he even braved a violent storm to fetch the midwife. So pleased was the woman's father that he told the priest that this brownie must be baptized. When the brownie next came into the house, the priest poured holy water over him. With a fearful shriek the brownie disappeared, never to be seen again.

Treat brownies with respect or they may show the tormenting, mischievous side of their fairy character, and become boggarts. One hardworking brownie was angered when his master criticized him for not stacking the corn well. As a result, that night, he threw it over a crag several miles away and deserted the farm where he had been so unappreciated.

THE MILKY WAY

Long ago people explained natural phenomena by means of fairy tales, such as this charming story from Estonia.

Once there was a beautiful fairy maiden named Lindu who guided all the birds of passage. Her charms attracted many suitors, among them the Pole Star. He came down from heaven in his many-jewelled cloak to woo her. However, she rejected him because he always had to remain in the same place in the sky.

The Moon was her next suitor. Light surrounded him whenever he moved, but she rejected him, too, saying that she could not marry anyone whose face changed so often.

After him came the Sun. As he walked flowers sprang up, corn turned golden and birds sang fit to burst their lungs. Nevertheless, she would not accept him for she said he always trod the same road.

Finally the Northern Lights descended, radiating streamers of light from his beautiful face. Lindu instantly fell in love with him and he with her. He left her to prepare her wedding clothes, saying he would soon return.

Alas, he never came back and Lindu wandered the earth dressed in her bridal attire and veil. In the end her father, the great Uko in the sky, took pity on her and lifted her up to the heavens. When you see the Milky Way, it is Lindu's wedding veil streaming across the sky. The story has a happy ending for she found the Northern Lights again and they often dance together from horizon to horizon, her veil guiding the birds of the world forever.

FAIRY RINGS

You may have seen fairy rings – circles of darker green grass – in a field. In folklore these are held to be fairy places, believed to mark the spot where fairies dance, or to grow above an underground fairy palace.

Human beings should treat them with respect, for if you were to sit inside one on Midsummer Eve or Hallowe'en you might well be whisked off to fairyland. Run round one nine times on the night of a full moon and you will possibly hear the fairies talking. But you must run round in the direction of the sun – from east to west. If you run the other way, or 'widdershins', it will put you in the fairies' power.

There is danger in listening to the songs of fairies as they dance in their fairy ring, for a mortal can be lured to join the revels; once inside the ring, as if he had eaten fairy food or kissed a fairy maiden, he can be rescued only with the greatest difficulty.

You will find it impossible to get rid of fairy rings on your land, despite the fact that there is a prosaic botanical explanation for them (they are caused by fungus growths). Even if you plough them up they will reappear, and you will have made an enemy of the fairies for life!

Dwarfs are the 'little men' who live underground – in hills, caves, down mines and in the clefts of rocks. Some stories say that if they venture above ground during daylight they will be transformed into stones, while others claim that they turn into toadstools between dawn and dusk. Living underground, many dwarfs become miners; others are skilful at working metals. These occupations also give them the reputation of being strong and possessing strong appetites.

Dwarfs are, on the whole, helpful to men even though their ugly appearance might make you think the contrary. In one Swiss story the kindly dwarfs often did men's hard and heavy work during the night. Early in the morning the dwarfs would hide in the bushes and laugh as the astonished country people saw their work was already done. One inquisitive shepherd tried to find out who was responsible and he put ashes down on the ground hoping the footprints would reveal who the mysterious workers were. The dwarfs, offended by his meddling, left the village, and some say they never again helped mankind.

In a hill near Brunswick in Germany lived another group of well-disposed dwarfs. If any of the local people needed festive clothes, party dishes or other special items, they would knock on the hill saying: 'Before the sun is up tomorrow, at the hill shall be the things we borrow.' And sure enough, whatever they had asked for would be on the hillside next morning. All the dwarfs asked for in payment was a little food from the feast.

FAIRY HABITATS

Fairies have many different types of home. Some live in woods in mountains; underground in caves or down mines; in the air or under water. Fairies are found in all these places because of the belief in folklore that fairies were originally fallen angels who, on their downward journey from heaven, took up residence on the earth wherever they could find shelter.

However, there are some habitats which are more popular with the fairies than others. One such is inside hollow hills. Fairies living here are held to be the spirits of the dead and the hollow hills are, in fact, ancient barrows or burial mounds.

Fairies furnish the interiors of these hills with whatever they find lying on the hillside or with household utensils they have 'borrowed' from humans. Sometimes they may be like Hans Andersen's description in his story 'The Elf Hill', where 'the floor was washed with moonshine, the walls rubbed down with fairy butter, so that they shone like the petals of tulip held up to the light'. This dwelling even had curtains 'hung up and made fast with snail slime'.

Fairies hold their revels in these hollow hills. Sometimes they remove the top of the hill and dance in the moonlight. Other hill-tops are elevated on pillars so that on certain nights bright lights shine out to entice passers-by to enter the fairyland. It is possible, however, to find the entrance to this dwelling by walking nine times round the fairy hill on the night of a full moon.

Nevertheless, not all fairy dwellings are fixed in one place. The Peris, the Persian good fairies, frequently transport their amber and gold palaces across the plains of Persia.

Islands have a unique enchantment, and perhaps this is why many mysterious islands have long been held to belong to the fairies. Fairy islands are believed to lie to the west of Europe, and have a variety of names – Isles of the Blest, Fortunate Isles, Land of the Young, Land of the Living and the Plain of Happiness.

Fairy islands are elusive, often shrouded in mist, and can only be glimpsed momentarily. Some appear only once a year, at dawn on Easter Day; others, like the Celtic Hy Brasail, are only seen once in seven years. One island was frequently sighted from the Canary Islands, with its peaks and promontories clearly defined. But according to the American writer Washington Irving, whenever sailors approached the place it melted away.

Islands are frequently described as the true land of fairy, made of crystal and gold and beautiful beyond belief. They enjoy perpetual spring and are regions of peace and plenty where the fairies can feast, dance and hunt undisturbed. The inhabitants even take part in battles, and those who are killed rise up healed the next day to fight again. This is why the legendary King Arthur was taken to the magic Western Isle of Avalon, 'where falls not hail or rain or any snow', after his final battle to recover from his wounds.

The legends attached to these islands may originally have arisen because strange plants, trees, nuts and other objects were often washed ashore in the Azores, the Hebrides and Portugal. But in 1508 a French ship is said actually to have encountered a boatload of American Indians off the coast of England, an event that no doubt reinforced the belief in magic isles across the sea.

Many old fairy beliefs have lingered on into this century. Children still put their milk teeth under the pillow so that a fairy can change them into coins overnight. People who do not put a star at the top of their Christmas tree probably have a fairy doll instead – a custom which originated in Germany. The fairy doll in this case symbolizes an angel. A popular Christmas treat for children is a visit to J. M. Barrie's play *Peter Pan*, during which they will be asked if they believe in fairies. The answer is always enthusiastically affirmative, in order to save the life of Peter Pan's friend Tinkerbell, the will-o'-the-wisp-like fairy.

Every now and then new instances of fairies are reported. During the First World War there were the gremlins, malevolent little spirits who lived in the engines of aeroplanes and could prevent the safe return of British pilots. More recently a London woman claimed that she often heard fairies talking, and she described their voices as sounding like a speeded-up tape recording.

Fairies have even been photographed too. In 1917 two young sisters from Cottingley in the north of England claimed that they had seen and talked to fairies in their garden. Their father took photographs and, to the astonishment of all, tiny winged creatures appeared on the photographic plates. They still appeared when photographs were taken under controlled conditions. Many eminent men believed them to be genuine, among them Sir Arthur Conan Doyle, creator of the detective Sherlock Holmes. A firm believer in fairies, he set out his beliefs in a book called *The Coming of the Fairies.*

However, as to the Cottingley fairies, they would, perhaps, have been more convincing if they had not been wearing contemporary dress and hairstyles.

THE DEPARTURE OF THE FAIRIES

Fairies have always been a race with a reputation for moving on. Sometimes they are driven away by too much human interference, as in the case of the *Heinzelmännchen*. These Teutonic house fairies were frightened away by a zealous housewife who was so determined to catch them that she scattered dried peas on the stairs to make them trip up. The fairies immediately collected their belongings and left the house.

Early in the nineteenth century a little boy and his sister witnessed the dwarfs leaving Scotland. Mounted on tiny horses with all their belongings they rode away in broad daylight. As they passed, the last dwarf told the children that 'the People of Peace shall never more be seen in Scotland'.

Sometimes fairy migrations are only to another part of the country but other fairies have journeyed across continents. Some fairies even reached America by travelling 'on the boots of the Pilgrim Fathers' and this explains why there are common characteristics between the activities of fairies found in America and Europe.

Therefore, it is not surprising to find that fairies have travelled to Australia. Here one immigrant Scottish family forgot to leave out the usual cup for the fairies when they brewed some prohibited liquor. The affronted fairies led the customs officer to the illicit still, and he confiscated all their brew.

ACKNOWLEDGEMENTS

Of the many books which have provided source material for *Fairies* the most valuable were:

Dictionary of Fairies, Katharine Briggs (Allen Lane, 1976)
Mythology of Fairies, Thomas Keightley (London, 1828)
Fairies, exhibition catalogue (Brighton Museum, 1980)

Illustrations

The author and publishers wish to thank the following for permission to reproduce illustrations and photographs: *Ring A Ring O'Fairies* by Madeleine Nightingale (Basil Blackwell), page 33; *The Brownies at Home* by Palmer Cox (The Century Company, 1893), page 41; *Green Willow* by Grace James (MacMillan, 1926), page 43; *Down-Adown-Derry* by Walter de la Mare (Constable, 1922), pages 5 and 49; Cooper-Bridgeman Library, pages 7, 26-27 and 55; Peter Cope, page 23 and jacket; Mary Evans Picture Library, pages 11, 17, 19, 28, 38-39, 45, 47 and 51; *Norse Fairy Tales* by P.C. Asbjornsen and J.I. Moe (S.T. Freeman, 1910), page 13; Michael Holford, pages 25 and 31; John Johnson Collection, Oxford, page 35; Jeremy Maas Gallery, pages 15, 21, 29 and 53; *Fairy Mythology* by Thomas Keightley (Alister Mathews, 1828), page 9; Phillips, page 3; Pictures of Past Times, page 37.